THE ROSARY
FOR CHILDREN

Nihil Obstat: Reverend Michael L. Diskin, Assistant Chancellor
Imprimatur: Most Reverend Thomas J. Ol_____ _____
Date: March 18, 20__

By Bart Tesori_

Illustrated by Migue_

catholic children's CLASSICS

ISBN 978-1-61796-163-2

2

The Story of the Rosary

The Rosary is a very special prayer! When we pray the Rosary, we think about events in the lives of Jesus and Mary. We call these events "Mysteries," because they teach us something about the love of God. As we pray, we open up our hearts to Jesus and Mary, and we let them teach us.

A long time ago, monks prayed the 150 Psalms as part of their daily prayer. Catholics who worked and had families wanted to pray too, so they replaced the Psalms with the Our Father, the Hail Mary, and the Glory Be. They kept count using a Rosary, which is a string of beads from which hangs a crucifix.

This book will help you to pray and reflect on the Mysteries of the Rosary. You will find something to think about for each of the Mysteries. You will see how much God loves you and how special Our Blessed Mother Mary is.

Saint John Paul II said that when we pray the Rosary, we are praying it in union with people all over the world, even those who have died. Each prayer of the Rosary is like a rose we offer to Our Lady. As we pray the Rosary, our fingers on the beads draw us closer to the crucifix, and our hearts draw us closer to Jesus.

How to Pray the Rosary

- Make the *Sign of the Cross* and pray the *Apostles' Creed*, while holding the crucifix.
- Pray one *Our Father* on the first bead, three *Hail Marys* on the next three beads for the virtues of Faith, Hope, and Charity, and finish with a *Glory Be*.
- Announce the first Mystery. Pause for a moment to think about it. Then pray an *Our Father* on the Our Father bead, ten *Hail Marys* on the next ten beads, and finish with a *Glory Be*. This is one decade.
- If you wish, pray the *Fatima Prayer* (found on page 29) after the *Glory Be*.
- Continue in this way until all you have prayed all five decades. To finish, pray the *Hail Holy Queen* and the *Prayer after the Rosary (found on page 27)*.

There are 20 mysteries of the Rosary. We usually pray the **Joyful Mysteries** of the Rosary on Mondays and Saturdays. We pray the **Luminous Mysteries** on Thursdays. We pray the **Sorrowful Mysteries** on Tuesdays and Fridays. We pray the **Glorious Mysteries** on Wednesdays and Sundays.

Let us now reflect on the different Mysteries of the Rosary.

The Joyful Mysteries

1. The Annunciation

In the village of Nazareth lived a lovely young lady named Mary. Mary was filled with grace from the first moment of life in her mother's womb. She was engaged to be married to a carpenter named Joseph.

One day, the angel Gabriel appeared to Mary. He said, "Do not be afraid, Mary, for you have found favor with God. You will give birth to a son, and you shall call Him Jesus. He will be great, and He will be called the Son of the Most High God." Mary said, "Let it be done unto me according to your word."

2. The Visitation of Mary to Her Cousin Elizabeth

Gabriel told Mary that her elderly cousin Elizabeth was also going to have a baby. This made Mary very happy. Mary hurried to the hill country where Elizabeth and her husband Zechariah lived.

When Elizabeth heard Mary's voice, the baby inside her jumped for joy! Elizabeth felt thrilled that the mother of God would visit her. "Blessed are you among women and blessed is the fruit of your womb!" she exclaimed. In response, Mary sang, "My soul proclaims the greatness of the Lord, and my spirit rejoices in God my savior."

3. The Birth of Jesus

The Roman Emperor decreed that a census should be taken of all the people. Joseph and Mary journeyed to Bethlehem, the city of David. There in a little stable among the lowly animals, Jesus was born. Angels appeared to shepherds in the nearby fields, singing, "Glory to God in the highest and on earth peace to those on whom his favor rests."

4. The Presentation of Jesus

Not long after Jesus was born, Mary and Joseph went to Jerusalem to present Him in the temple. God had promised Simeon that he would not die until he had seen the Messiah. Simeon blessed Jesus, and told Mary that Jesus would bring about the fall and rise of many in Israel. He said, "A sword will pierce your own soul as well, so that the thoughts of many hearts may be revealed."

5. The Finding of Jesus in the Temple

When Jesus was 12, Joseph and Mary took Him to Jerusalem for the Passover, as they did every year. They returned home, but Jesus stayed behind without telling His parents. Mary and Joseph spent three days looking for Him. They found Jesus in the temple speaking to the elders. Mary asked, "Son, why have You done this to us?" Jesus answered, "Did you not know that I must be in my Father's house?" Then Jesus returned home and was obedient to His parents.

The Luminous Mysteries

1. The Baptism in the Jordan

John the Baptist baptized people in the Jordan River. He told them to turn away from sin. "Repent," he said, "for the kingdom of heaven is at hand." When Jesus came to be baptized, John exclaimed: "Behold the Lamb of God!" After John baptized Jesus, a voice from heaven said, "This is My beloved Son, with whom I am well pleased." The Holy Spirit came upon Jesus like a dove and led Him into the wilderness. Jesus fasted and prayed for forty days. He overcame temptation and the devil. Jesus was then ready to begin His work.

2. The Wedding at Cana

Mary, Jesus, and the disciples were invited to a wedding in the village of Cana in Galilee. During the feast, the newlyweds ran out of wine. Mary told Jesus, "They have no wine." She told the servers, "Do whatever He tells you."

At the feast, there were six stone jars filled with water for washing. Jesus told the servers to fill them to the brim and to bring some to the wine steward. The steward was amazed at what he tasted. The water had become wine—the best he had ever drunk. This was Jesus' first miracle, and His disciples began to believe in Him.

3. The Proclamation of the Kingdom

Jesus began preaching to the people. He said, "The kingdom of God is at hand. Repent and believe in the Gospel!" For three years Jesus showed God's love to the people by teaching them, healing them, and driving out demons.

4. The Transfiguration

One day, Jesus took Peter, James, and John with Him up onto a high mountain. While Jesus was praying, His face started to shine like the sun and His clothes became dazzling white. Then two men—Moses and Elijah—appeared next to Jesus. A voice spoke from a cloud. "This is my beloved Son. Listen to Him." Moses and Elijah disappeared, and Jesus was again alone with His disciples.

5. The Gift of the Eucharist

On the night before He died, Jesus and His Apostles shared their last supper together. Jesus knew that He would give His life the next day for the sins of the world. However, before He died, Jesus wanted to give us the gift of Himself in the sacrament of His Body and His Blood. Jesus took the bread, blessed it, and said, "Take and eat, all of you. This is My Body." Then, taking the chalice filled with wine, He said, "This cup is the new covenant in My Blood, shed for you. Do this in remembrance of Me."

The Sorrowful Mysteries

1. The Agony in the Garden

After supper, Jesus and His Apostles went to the Garden of Gethsemane to pray. He took Peter, James, and John with Him a bit further. He told them, "My soul is sorrowful unto death. Remain here and keep watch with Me." Then Jesus prayed, "My Father, if it is possible, let this cup pass from me; yet not as I will, but as you will." When Jesus returned, He found His disciples asleep. He asked them, "Could you not watch one hour with Me?" Just then, Judas, one of the disciples, appeared. He betrayed Jesus with a kiss. The soldiers arrested Jesus and took Him away.

2. The Scourging at the Pillar

The soldiers took Jesus to stand trial before the chief priests and religious leaders of the Jewish people. The high priest questioned Jesus and his officers struck Jesus. They wanted Him to be killed for the crimes that they said He had committed. The next morning, they brought Jesus to Pontius Pilate, the Roman governor, for questioning. Pilate found no fault in Him, but to satisfy the leaders, he ordered that Jesus be tied to a post and whipped. Jesus was covered with deep cuts all over His body. This fulfilled what the prophet Isaiah had prophesied: "By his wounds we were healed."

3. The Crowning with Thorns

The soldiers placed a scarlet robe on Jesus to mock Him. They put a crown of thorns on His head and knelt before Him. They said, "Hail, King of the Jews!" They hit Jesus over the head, which hurt Him very much. Then they took Jesus back to Pontius Pilate. Pilate brought Jesus out and said to the crowd, "Behold the man!" He thought that they might change their minds and let Jesus live. But the people cried out, "Crucify Him!"

4. The Carrying of the Cross

The soldiers made Jesus carry the cross up Mount Calvary, where He would be crucified. Jesus was beaten so badly that He could barely walk. The soldiers were afraid that Jesus would die on the way. They forced Simon of Cyrene to carry the cross behind Jesus.

5. The Crucifixion

When they reached the hill of Calvary, the soldiers crucified Jesus. Mother Mary and Saint John stood at the foot of the cross. Mary heard Jesus pray, "Father, forgive them, for they know not what they do." Jesus gave Mary to John. Then Jesus gave John to His mother Mary. Jesus cried, "It is finished! Father, into Your hands I commit My spirit." Then He bowed His head, and died.

The Glorious Mysteries

1. The Resurrection

Very early in the morning of the third day, an earthquake shook the ground and an angel rolled away the stone from the tomb of Jesus. He looked like lightening and his clothing was white as snow. The guards ran away in fear. Meanwhile, Mary Magdalene and some women had gone to the tomb to anoint the body of Jesus. The angel told the women, "He is not here. He has risen as He said. Go, tell His disciples!"

2. The Ascension

After the Resurrection, Jesus appeared to His disciples. He spoke to Mary Magdalene who had come to His tomb. He walked with two disciples to the village of Emmaus, but they did not recognize Him. Jesus revealed Himself to them— first in the Scriptures and then in the breaking of the bread.

Jesus appeared to His Apostles when they were gathered in a locked room. He gave them the Holy Spirit and the power to forgive sins. Jesus later met some of His disciples by the Sea of Tiberias. At the end of 40 days, Jesus blessed his Apostles. He sent them out into the world to preach the Gospel and baptize in the name of the Father, the Son, and the Holy Spirit. Then the Lord Jesus, after He spoke to them, was taken up to heaven and took His seat at the right hand of God.

3. The Descent of the Holy Spirit

Before He returned to heaven, Jesus promised His apostles that the Holy Spirit would come upon them in power. While Mary and the disciples were gathered in one place praying and waiting, suddenly, on the feast of Pentecost, a noise like a rushing mighty wind came from heaven and filled the whole house. There appeared to them tongues as of fire, which parted and came to rest on each one of them. And they were all filled with the Holy Spirit and began to speak in different languages, as the Spirit enabled them to proclaim. The Apostles were finally ready to spread the Gospel.

4. The Assumption of Mary into Heaven

After Jesus returned to heaven, the apostle John cared for Mother Mary for many years. When her earthly life was over, the Virgin Mary was taken up body and soul into heaven. We believe that one day, like Mary, our bodies and souls will also be reunited in heaven.

5. The Crowning of Mary as Queen of Heaven

In heaven, Jesus honored His Mother Mary in a special way. He crowned her as Queen of heaven and earth, Queen of all the angels and saints! Mary is also the Mother of the whole Church. From heaven, Mary continues to comfort and console all of her children. The angels and saints joyfully proclaim, "Hail Holy Queen!"

The Prayers of the Rosary

The Apostles' Creed

I believe in God, the Father almighty,
Creator of heaven and earth,
and in Jesus Christ, his only Son, our Lord,
who was conceived by the Holy Spirit,
born of the Virgin Mary,
suffered under Pontius Pilate,
was crucified, died, and was buried.

He descended into hell;
on the third day
he rose again from the dead;
he ascended into heaven,
and is seated at the right hand
of God the Father almighty;
from there he will come to judge
the living and the dead.

I believe in the Holy Spirit,
the holy catholic Church,
the communion of saints,
the forgiveness of sins,
the resurrection of the body,
and life everlasting. Amen.

24

Our Father

Our Father, who art in heaven,
hallowed be Thy name.
Thy kingdom come, Thy will be done,
on earth as it is in heaven.

Give us this day our daily bread;
and forgive us our trespasses,
as we forgive those who trespass against us;
and lead us not into temptation,
but deliver us from evil. Amen.

Hail Mary

Hail Mary, full of grace,
the Lord is with thee.
Blessed art thou among women,
and blessed is the fruit
of thy womb, Jesus.

Holy Mary, Mother of God,
pray for us sinners,
now and at the hour of our death. Amen.

Glory Be

Glory be to the Father, and to the Son,
and to the Holy Spirit; as it was in the beginning,
is now, and ever shall be, world without end. Amen.

Hail, Holy Queen

Hail, Holy Queen, Mother of Mercy,
Our life, our sweetness, and our hope!
To thee do we cry,
poor banished children of Eve;
to thee do we send up our sighs,
mourning and weeping in this valley of tears.
Turn then, most gracious advocate,
thine eyes of mercy towards us;
and after this our exile, show unto us
the blessed fruit of thy womb, Jesus;
O clement, O loving, O sweet Virgin Mary.

Prayer after the Rosary

O God, Whose only begotten Son, by His Life, Death, and Resurrection, has purchased for us the rewards of eternal life: grant, we beseech You, that, meditating upon these mysteries of the Most Holy Rosary of the Blessed Virgin Mary, we may imitate what they contain and obtain what they promise, through the same Christ our Lord. Amen.

Fatima Prayer

O my Jesus, forgive us our sins;

save us from the fires of hell.

Lead all souls to Heaven,

especially those most in need of Your mercy.

The Memorare

Remember, O most gracious Virgin Mary,

that never was it known, that anyone who fled

to thy protection, implored thy help,

or sought thy intercession, was left unaided.

Inspired by this confidence,

I fly unto thee, O Virgin of virgins my Mother.

To thee do I come, before thee I stand,

sinful and sorrowful.

O Mother of the Word Incarnate,

despise not my petitions,

but in thy mercy hear and answer me. Amen.

The Promises of the Rosary

Our Blessed Mother Mary appeared to the children at Lourdes and Fatima with a Rosary in her hands. She calls us to pray the Rosary daily. According to tradition, our Lady gave promises about the Rosary to Saint Dominic. Here are some of them:

1. Whoever serves me by praying the Rosary will receive special graces from God.
2. I promise my special protection and graces.
3. The Rosary shall be a powerful armor against hell.
4. The Rosary will help good works to grow. It will obtain abundant mercy from God.
5. Those who give themselves to me by praying the Rosary shall not perish.
6. Whoever prays the Rosary devoutly and reflects on the Mysteries shall never be overcome by misfortune.
7. Whoever has a true devotion for the Rosary shall not die without the Sacraments of the Church.
8. You shall obtain all you ask of me by praying the Rosary.
9. All those who spread the Holy Rosary shall be aided by me in their necessities.
10. All who pray the Rosary are my children, and brothers and sisters to my only Son Jesus Christ.
11. Devotion to my Rosary is a great sign that you will be with me someday in heaven.